SONG DOGS!

R.O.C.K. IN THE U.S.A.

by Laura Parris

A dog walker's "client" pawtraits highlighted with Song Title captions!

BookSurge Publishing
7290B Investment Dr
North Charleston, SC 29418

Library of Congress Control Number: 2009911285

ISBN: 1-4392-6385-X

Printed in the United States of America

SONG DOGS! is available at www.amazon.com and www.laurasgiftstudio.com

Lightning

GET THE PARTY STARTED

Charlie

I'M WALKIN'

Bailey

SHARP DRESSED MAN

Riley O.

HARVEST MOON

Arthur

CRY LIKE A BABY

Ivory & Hershey

STAND BY YOUR MAN

Frankie & Cappuccino

THE BOYS ARE BACK IN TOWN

BABY COME BACK

Cassie

FOREVER IN BLUE JEANS

DO YA THINK I'M SEXY?

Bernie

HUNGRY FOR LOVE

JUMPIN' JACK FLASH

Loope & Chello

WE WILL ROCK YOU

Rocco

I'M SO EXCITED

Bella P.

GO AWAY LITTLE GIRL

SURF CITY

Copper

COAT OF MANY COLORS

WE ARE THE CHAMPIONS

Cosmo

MY BOY LOLLIPOP

Cooper & Sydney

WHITE WEDDING

Diva

SECRET GARDEN

TURNING JAPANESE

Tammy

HARD HABIT TO BREAK

YOU LIGHT UP MY LIFE

Phoenix

BRAND NEW TOY

REBEL REBEL

Cody

R.O.C.K. IN THE U.S.A.

COWBOY TAKE ME AWAY

Buddy

UP ON CRIPPLE CREEK

YOU MAKE ME FEEL LIKE DANCING

Cindy & Noelle

GIRLS JUST WANT TO HAVE FUN

SUITE: JUDY BLUE EYES

Theodore

I WANT YOU TO WANT ME

NEW KID IN TOWN

Millie

GOLDEN YEARS

DARLING BE HOME SOON

Dina

COME ON GET HAPPY

I ONLY HAVE EYES FOR YOU

Jakey

PRINCE OF TIDES

BROWN EYED HANDSOME MAN

Peanut

AIN'T SHE SWEET

WHY CAN'T WE BE FRIENDS

I'LL BE YOUR BABY TONIGHT

BASKETBALL JONES

Lace

DON'T IT MAKE MY BROWN EYES BLUE

Sprocket

ANTICIPATION

Juno

GLAD ALL OVER

ICEMAN

Primo

HUNGRY LIKE THE WOLF

Shaina

WHERE TIME STANDS STILL

Sonny

BEAUTIFUL BOY

WAITING ON A FRIEND

Nina

THREE TIMES A LADY

I PUT A SPELL ON YOU

Tini & Dora

SISTERS OF THE MOON

Benji

FUN FUN FUN

Jesse

I FEEL PRETTY

Splash

COUNTRY COMFORT

Delilah

ANGELS WITH DIRTY FACES

Barney

FREEZE FRAME

Bauer

GETTING TO KNOW YOU

Ziggy

COME ON DOWN TO MY BOAT

Shayna

SIMPLY IRRESISTIBLE

Riley & Frisco

BEST FRIENDS

Corgi

HERE COMES THE SUN

Cooper

ON THE ROAD AGAIN

Reina

WILD THING

YOU'RE A GOOD MAN, CHARLIE BROWN

Opus

REBEL YELL

SUPERWOMAN

Jagger

ME AND MY ARROW

DON'T FENCE ME IN

Roxxy

WITCHY WOMAN

Mara

PRETTY LITTLE ANGEL EYES

Sara

MRS. BROWN YOU'VE GOT A LOVELY DAUGHTER

Samson & Marlow

HE AIN'T HEAVY, HE'S MY BROTHER

Samantha

SHE'S GOT A WAY

YUMMY YUMMY YUMMY

Abby

SAD EYES

Harley

IS SHE REALLY GOING OUT WITH HIM?

Lilly

WORKING MY WAY BACK TO YOU

Hannibal

THE BOXER

Goliath

SIT DOWN I THINK I LOVE YOU

Jackson & Mazzy

CHAPEL OF LOVE

Lester

A PLACE IN THE SUN

Jack

INCENSE AND PEPPERMINTS

Snowy & Heidi

EBONY AND IVORY

Shadow

STOP THIEF

Sebastian & Niki

HAPPY TOGETHER

Nakita

STILL CRAZY AFTER ALL THESE YEARS

Lil Moe

WOOLY BULLY

WEREWOLVES OF LONDON

Rex

BLINDED BY THE LIGHT

Lexi

RIGHT HERE WAITING

RILEY F.

WALK ON THE WILD SIDE

Nemo

RAMBLIN' MAN

Ricky

LOVE SHACK

SONG DOGS! is dedicated to all the amazing animal rescue workers for all of their selfless efforts. Part of the proceeds from this book project will be donated to Forgotten Friends of Long Island Inc. (www.forgottenfriendsoflongisland.org) SONG DOGS! is also dedicated to songwriters, artists and musicians for the magic they bring to the world!!

Special thanks to all my dog walking/pet sitting customers for allowing me to hang out with their pets and have such great fun! I love my furry clients and they inspire me greatly!

Heartfelt thanks to Kevin Swift, my husband and partner in The Purrfect Pet Sitters, LLC, for all his patience and support. Many thanks to my sons Dylan and Donovan Swift for all of their helpful suggestions during the making of this book.

Other Titles available by Laura Parris:
SONG CATS! - A pet sitter's favorite feline photos highlighted with Song Title captions. BookSurge Publishing, available at **www.amazon.com and www.laurasgiftstudio.com** Part of the proceeds of SONG CATS! will be donated to a cat rescue organization.

Titles Coming Soon by Laura Parris include:
SONG CATS! - Stray Cat Strut - A dogwalker's photo gallery of the homeless cats encountered along her dog walking route. Photos are highlighted with Song Title captions. A portion of the proceeds of the book project will go to an animal rescue organization.
SONG BIRDS & MORE! - A dogwalker/petsitter's photos of the wonderful wildlife seen during her dog walking & petsitting adventures. Song Titles serve as photo captions. A portion of the proceeds of this book project will benefit a charity.
SONG 'SCAPES! - A dogwalker's pics of the beautiful everyday landscapes that are her workplace. Song Titles act as photo captions. A portion of the proceeds of this book project will benefit a charity.

For more photo gifts visit www.laurasgiftstudio.com
For information about our pet care services visit www.thepurrfectpetsitters.com

About the Author: Laura lives with her husband and two sons on Long Island, NY along with 1 dog, 12 cats and a chinchilla. A former singer/songwriter and record business employee, music has always played a huge part in her life. She found herself singing to her "clients" often and hence the idea for this book was born. Laura graduated from SUNY Stonybrook and then attended Hofstra Law School for a year but decided this was not the right career path. She started Laura's Gift Studio, LLC in 2004 as an outlet for her creativity and The Purrfect Pet Sitters, LLC with her husband in 2006 to make a career out of caring for animals.

Made in the USA
Charleston, SC
25 November 2009